HÄNSEL
AND
GRETEL

HÄNSEL
AND
GRETEL
Vocal Score

ENGELBERT
HUMPERDINCK

DOVER PUBLICATIONS, INC.
Mineola, New York

Hansel and Gretel in Full Score
is available in Dover edition 0-486-28818-8

Bibliographical Note

This Dover edition, first published in 2004, is an unabridged republication of the work first published by B. Schott's Söhne, Mainz, 1895 [plate no. 25788].

International Standard Book Number: 0-486-43826-0

Manufactured in the United States of America
Dover Publications, Inc., 31 East 2nd Street, Mineola, N.Y., 11501

CONTENTS

Hänsel and Gretel

a Fairy Opera

In three Acts by Adelheid Wette

Translated and adapted into English

by

Constance Bache

The Music composed by

E. Humperdinck

Complete Vocal Score by R. Kleinmichel   net Pr.

   id.   Pianoforte Solo   id.   net Pr.

   id.   Pianoforte Duet   id.   net Pr.

Copyright for all countries.

SCHOTT & Cº
159 Regent Street.
LONDON

B. SCHOTT'S SÖHNE
Weihergarten 5.
MAYENCE

SCHOTT FRERES
82 Montagne de la Cour.
BRUXELLES

EDITIONS SCHOTT
Boul⁴ Malesherbes (40 Rue d'Anjou)
PARIS

Printed in Germany.

[Original title page]

Hänsel and Gretel.

Dramatis Personæ.

Peter, a broom-maker.. *Baritone.*
Gertrude, his wife... *Mezzo-Soprano.*
Hänsel } .... *Mezzo-Soprano.*
Gretel } their children
.... *Soprano.*
The Witch who eats children............................. *Mezzo-Soprano.*
Sandman (the sleep fairy).. *Soprano.*
Dewman (the dawn fairy)... *Soprano.*
Children.. *Sopranos and Contraltos.*

Fourteen Angels .... *Ballet.*

First Act.   Home.
Second Act.   The forest.
Third Act.   The witch's house.

Hänsel and Gretel.

Once upon a time there was a poor couple, a broom-maker and his wife, who had two children; the boy was called Hänsel, and the girl Gretel. One day the parents had gone tramping over the country to try and dispose of their goods. On leaving the children the mother had given them the last bit of bread that was in the house, and had told them to be very industrious while she was away.

It was not long before the lively children tired of their work, and began to get hungry, till Hänsel was on the point of crying, when Gretel came to the rescue and cheered him up again. So they sang and danced till they both forgot their hunger and work, and at last in tremendous spirits they tumbled over one another on the floor.

Now it happened that just at this moment the mother came home again, tired and out of sorts, for she had not taken a single farthing, and consequently had brought home nothing to eat. When she found the children sitting on the floor and making ever such a noise, instead of being quietly at their work, she got very angry and drove them out with blows into the wood hard by. They were not to come back until they had filled their basket with strawberries. Then she sank wearily down on a chair, and dropped asleep from hunger and fatigue.

The children soon got happy again over their strawberry picking, and did not notice that they were losing their way and getting deeper and deeper into the wood, until at last they halted by the Ilsenstein.

Full of fun and high spirits they imitated the cuckoo's cry, and accused him of turning his little ones out of their nest and eating the eggs of other birds. And as they imitated him in this, making the strawberries take the place of the eggs, their basket unawares got empty.

Meanwhile it got gradually dark, and the children became frightened. They could not find their way, and wandered helplessly around. The wood seemed full of ghosts, and the trees rustled in an uncanny fashion. The birds were all silent, and only the cuckoo was still heard in the far distance. But from the Ilsenstein there arose queer shapes in the mist, so that the poor lonely children were frightened out of their wits. They cowered under a great fir-tree to try to find shelter from the terrors of the night, until the Sand-man, who comes at night to strew sand over people's eyes to send them to sleep, appeared and quieted them with kindly gestures. Then, after they had said their usual evening prayer to the fourteen angels, they lay down and went to sleep on the soft moss. And the fourteen angels hovered around and watched over the good children so that no harm might come to them.

The next morning they were awakened from their dreams by the little Dew-man, whose business it is to run over the hills and fields awakening everything that is still slumbering. And what should they see before them but a little house all made of cakes and sugar-candy, and glistening in the light of the sun, and smelling so delicious that the hungry children, who could scarely believe their eyes, were quite wild with delight.

They cautiously approached the cottage, and as they did not see anybody about they became bolder, and broke a piece off the wall, which tasted exceedingly nice. At this moment a voice was heard from within the house, saying,

»Nibble, nibble, mousekin,

Who's nibbling at my housekin?«

At first they were rather alarmed, but they soon regained their courage, and called to one another that it was only

»The wind, the wind,

The heavenly wind,«

and went on nibbling. But the door of the cottage softly opened, and a very old and ugly woman came out of it. Now there was something very wicked about this old creature. She was a witch, who rode on a broomstick through the air at night, and in the daytime enticed little children into her sugar-house, where she popped them in the oven and made them into gingerbread, which she afterwards eat. She tried to be very friendly with Hänsel and Gretel, and coaxed them in with honeyed words.

However the children distrusted the horrible old woman, and tried to run away. Then the witch raised her magic wand and spell-bound them both, so that they were rooted to the spot. She next took Hänsel and shut him up in a stable, and fed him with almonds and raisins to make him fat. She was so delighted, when she had done this, that she seized a broomstick and rode wildly on it round her house. After that she called Gretel, and told her to look into the oven and see if the cakes were done. But Gretel was sharper than the witch, and saw through her little dodge, so she pretended to be very stupid, and begged the old woman to show her how it was to be done. The old woman unsuspectingly bent down over the oven to show Gretel what to do, and peeped in. No sooner had she done this, than the children gave her a good push and in she tumbled. They quickly shut the iron door, and left her to bake in her own oven, while they danced away in good earnest. Suddenly a crack was heard, and the magic oven fell to pieces with a loud crash. And behold! the gingerbreads, which were standing in a row round the cottage, were transformed into living, pretty children, who joyfully surrounded Hänsel and Gretel, and thanked them for their happy release.

And what joy when the sorrowing parents appeared, and Hänsel and Gretel rushed delightedly into their arms once more! Then all sadness and want were banished for ever, for in the sugar-cottage they had found all sorts of treasures which would make them happy and rich for the rest of their days. And they all thanked God, who had taken care of them in their great need!

Adelheid Wette.

Hänsel and Gretel.

Prelude.

Ruhige, nicht zu langsame Bewegung.
Andante con moto. (♩ = 69)

E. Humperdinck.

Allegro non troppo. Munter. (Die Halben ungefähr wie vorher die Viertel.)

6

8

First Act.

Home.

First Scene.

(A small and poorly furnished room. In the background a door; a small window near it, looking on to the forest. On the left a fireplace with chimney above it. On the walls are hanging brooms of various sizes. Hänsel is sitting by the door, making brooms, and Gretel opposite him by the fireplace, knitting a stocking.)

Gretel.

Su - sy, lit - tle Su - sy, pray what is the news?

The geese are running bare-foot be-cause they've no shoes!

The cobbler has leather and plen-ty to spare, Why can't he

make the poor goose a new— (continuing) pair?

Hänsel (interrupting her.)

Then they'll have to go bare-foot!

Hänsel.

Ei - a po-pei-a, pray what's to be

14

16

Hänsel (dancing round the room.)

When blanc-mange is an – y-where near, Then Hän - sel, Hän - sel,

Hän-sel is there! How thick is the cream on the milk, lets

(He licks the cream off his finger.)

taste it! O Ge - mi-ni, wouldn't I like to

Più animato.
Gretel.

(gives him a rap on his fingers.)

What, Hän-sel, tast-ing? Aren't you a - shamed? Out with your

drink it!
Più animato.

fingers quick, gree-dy boy! Go back to your work again, be

quick, that we may both have done in time! If mother comes and we haven't done

Tempo come prima

Hänsel (sticking

right, Then _ bad-ly it will fare with us to - night! Work a-gain?

his hands into his trousers pockets.)

poco ritard.

No, not for me! That's not my i - dea at all, It doesn't

a tempo

suit me! It's such a bore! Dancing is jol-li-er far,__ I'm

Gretel.

Danc - ing! Danc - ing! O yes, that's bet - ter far.

sure!

And sing a song to keep us in time! One that our grand - mother

used to sing us: Sing then, and dance in time to the sing - ing!

22

So that I may dance like you. **Gretel.** With your foot you tap tap tap,

With your hand you clap clap clap, Right foot first, Left foot then, Round about and

Hänsel. back a-gain! With your foot you tap tap tap, With your hand you clap clap clap,

Gretel. Right foot first, Left foot then, Round and back a-gain! That was ve-ry good indeed,

joy is dance and jol-li-ty, And all that kind of thing! What I en-joy is dance and

fact I like fri-vo-li-ty, And all that kind of thing! In fact I like fri-

jol-li-ty Love to have my fling, _____ I like fri-vo-li-ty, And

vo-li-ty, Love to have my fling, In fact I quite pre-fer fri-vo-li-ty, And

(pulls Hänsel along, and dances round him - - - - - -

all that kind of thing! Tra la la la la la la la la la la, tra la

all that kind of thing!

then gives him a push.)

la la la la la la la! Come and have a twirl, my dear-est Hän-sel, Come and have a

turn with me, I pray, Come here to me, come here to me, I'm sure you can't say

Hänsel (gruffly.)

Nay! Go a-way from me, go a-way from me, I'm much too proud for you! With

Gretel.

lit - tle girls I do not dance, And so, my dear, a - dieu! Go,

take me for a fool? With naugh-ty boys I do not dance, And so, my dear, a-

Hänsel. *poco ritard.* *Tempo.* **Gretel.**

dieu! Now don't be cross, you sil-ly goose, You'll see I'll make you dance! Tra la

(they dance as before)

la tra la la tra la la la la, tra la la tra la la tra la la! Come and have a

Hänsel.

Tra la

twirl, my dear-est Hän-sel, Come and have a turn, my dear-est Hans! Sing

la tra la la tra la la la la, tra la la tra la la tra la la! Sing

lu-sti - ly hur - rah, hur-rah! While I dance with you! And if the stockings

lu-sti - ly hur - rah, hur-rah! While I dance with you! And if the shoes are

are in holes, Why mother'll knit some new!

Come and have a

(They dance by turns as before.)

all in holes, Why mother'll buy some new! Trala la tra la la tra la la la la, tra la

twirl, my dear-est Hän-sel!

On-ly have a

la tra la la tra la la! Tra la la tra la la tra la la la la, tra la

(Then they seize each other's hands and dance round and round,

twirl, my dear-est Hänsel! Tra la la trala la, tra la la trala la, tra la

la trala la trala la la la, tra la la la la, tra la la la la, tra la

fp *fp* *fp*

quicker and quicker, until at last they lose their balance and tumble over one another onto the floor.) *string.*

la tra la la, trala la trala la, trala la trala la, trala la trala la, tra

la la la, trala la trala la, tra la trala la, trala la trala la, tra

string.

fp *fp* *cresc.* - - -

la!

la!

f *f* *ff*

Hr. Str.

ff

Scene II.

children, And make your id — le fing — ers ting — le!

(In her anger at the children she gives the milkjug a knock, which sends it clattering on to the floor.)

Gra-cious! There goes the jug all to pie-ces!

(weeping)

What now can I cook for sup-per?

(She looks at her skirt, down which

the milk is streaming.)

(Hänsel covertly titters.)

How, sau - cy how dare you

(Going with a stick after Hänsel, who is running out at the door.)

laugh? Wait, wait till the fa - ther comes home!

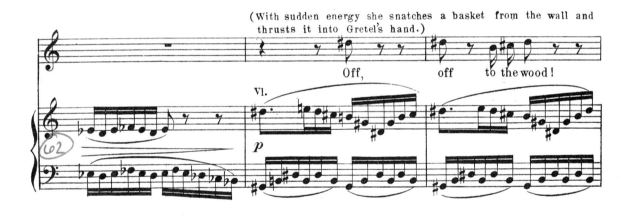

(With sudden energy she snatches a basket from the wall and thrusts it into Gretel's hand.)

Off, off to the wood!

there seek for straw - berries quick away! And if you don't

bring the bas-ket brim - ful I'll whip _ you so that you'll

(The children run into the forest.)

both _____ run a - way!

(She sits down by the table, exhausted.)

38

No crust in the cup - board
No milk in the pot,

(She rests her head on her hand.)

No, no - thing but wa - ter to drink!

Wea - ry am I, weary of liv - ing!

(Lays her head down on her arms and drops asleep.)

Father, send — help — to me! —

Scene III.

Commodo. ♩. = ♩   (A voice is heard in the distance)   **Father.**

Tra la la la, tra la la la, Lit-tle mo-ther, here am I! Tra la la la, tra la la la, Bringing luck and jol-li-ty!

(somewhat nearer)

1. Oh for you and me, poor mo-ther, Ev'-ry day is like the o-ther; With a big hole in the

pp Hr.(con Sordino)

Dble B.

Str.(con Sordino) *pp*

p

Vcl. *cresc.*

42

44

45

46

48

meanwhile packs away the things, lights a fire, breaks eggs into a saucepan, etc.)

Yon - der to the town I went, There was to be a great e - -vent,

Weddings, fairs and pre - pa - ra - tion For all kinds of ju - bi - la - tion!

Now's my chance to do some sel - ling,

So for that you may be thank - ful! He who

wants a feast to keep, He must scrub and brush and sweep,

52

So I brought my best goods out,

Tramped with them from house to house:

"Buy be - soms! good be - soms!

Buy my brush - es, sweep your car - pets, sweep your cob - webs!"

And so I drove a roar-ing trade, And sold my brush-es at the

high - - - - - est pri - - - ces!

54

55

56

59

An old witch with-in that wood doth dwell, And she's in league with the powers of hell. At mid-night hour, when nobody knows, A-way to the witches' dance ___ she goes. Up the chimney they fly, ___ on a broomstick they hie, ___

stalks a - round with a   crinch - ing, crunch - ing,   munch - ing sound,   and

children plump and   tender to eat   she lures with ma - gic   ginger-bread sweet.

Un poco più animato.

On e - - vil bent,   with

fell   intent   she   lures   the chil - dren, poor   little things, in the

(Prelude to the 2nd Act)

✠ Goes on to the "Witches' Ride."

The Witches' Ride.
Prelude to second Act.

66

Poco a poco più animato.

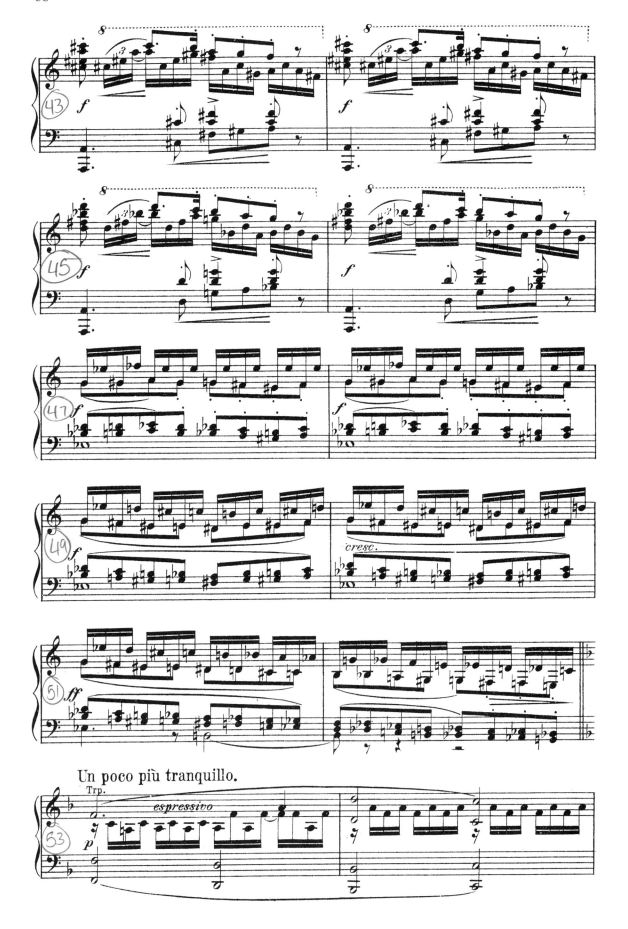

Un poco più tranquillo.

Un poco ritard.

(The curtain rises.)
Molto tranquillo.

(The middle of the forest. In the background

is the "Ilsenstein", thickly surrounded by fir-trees. On the right is a large fir-tree, under which Gretel is sitting on a mossy tree-trunk, and making a garland of wild roses. By her side lies a nose-gay of flowers. Amongst the bushes on the left is Hänsel, looking for strawberries. Sunset.)

Second Act.
In the forest.
Scene I.

Molto tranquillo. (♩ = 66)

Gretel (humming quietly to herself.)

There stands a lit-tle man in the wood a-lone, He wears a lit-tle man-tle of vel-vet brown, Say who can the mankin be, Standing there be-neath the tree, With the lit-tle man-tle of vel-vet brown? His hair is all of

gold, and his cheeks are red, He wears a lit-tle black cap up-on his

head, Say who can the mankin be, Standing there so si-lently, With the little

(She holds up the garland of roses and looks it all round)

black cap up-on his head?

With the little black cap up-on his

74

poco riten.

crown,   I give you the strawberries,   but   don't _____   eat them

poco riten.

Hr.   p   sf   dim.   pp

Tempo.

(He gives the basketful of strawberries into her other hand, at the same time kneeling before her

all!

Fl.

Cl.

dolce

Hr.

Hr.

in homage.)

Str.

Hr.
dim.   pp   *più p*

Gretel (roguishly.)

(At this moment a
cuckoo is heard.)   **Hänsel** (pointing with his hand.)

Cuckoo, cuckoo, where are you?

Cuckoo,   cuckoo, how are you?

Cuckoo-instrument (behind the scenes, heard as if quite in the distance.)

ppp

(A thick mist rises and completely hides the background.)

Scene II.

Moderato.

Sand-man (the Sleep-Fairy: strewing sand in the children's eyes.)
(with a soft gentle voice)

I shut the children's peep - ers, sh! And guard the lit - tle

sleep - ers, sh! For dear - ly do I love them, sh! And glad - ly watch a -

bove them, sh! And with my lit - tle bag of sand By

ev' - ry child's bed - side I stand; Then lit - tle tir - ed

90

hap - py dreams are sent you thro' the hours___ you sleep!

Hänsel (half asleep.) Gretel (ditto.)

Sand-man was there! Let us first say our evening - pray - er! (They cower down and fold their hands.)

L'istesso tempo.
Gretel. *mezza voce*

When at night I go to sleep, Fourteen an-gels watch do keep, Two my head are

Hänsel. *mezza voce*

When at night I go to sleep, Fourteen an-gels watch do keep, Two my head are

L'istesso tempo.

guard - ing, Two my feet are guid - ing, Two are on my right hand,

guard - ing, Two my feet are guid - ing, Two are on my

(Complete darkness.)

Tempo.

(Here a bright light

suddenly breaks through the mist, which forthwith rolls itself together into the form of a

Con espressione.

staircase vanishing in perspective in the middle of the stage.)

Scene III.

Pantomime.

Poco a poco più animato.

(Fourteen angels, in light floating garments, pass down the staircase two and two, at

intervals, while it is getting gradually lighter. The angels place themselves, according to the order mentioned in the evening hymn, around the sleeping children; the first couple at their heads

the second at their feet, the third on the right, the fourth on the left; then the fifth and sixth couples

distribute themselves amongst the other couples so that the circle of the angels is completed.)

(Lastly the seventh couple comes into the circle, and takes its place as "guardian angels" on each side of the children.)

96

(The remaining angels now join hands and dance a stately dance around the group.)

Tempo moderato.

(The whole stage is filled with an intense light.)

(Whilst the angels group themselves in a picturesque tableau the curtain slowly falls.)

Third Act.
The Witch's House.

Scene I.

(Scene the same as at the end of Act II. The background is still hidden in mist, which gradually rises during the following. The angels have vanished. Morning is breaking. The Dew-Fairy steps forward and shakes dewdrops from a blue-bell over the sleeping children.)

hours, — The scent of trees and flow-ers, Then up, ye sleep-ers a-

wa - - ken! The ro-sy dawn is smi -

ling, Then up, ye sleep-ers, a - wake, _____ a - -

(Hurries off singing. The children begin to stir.)

wake! _____

Un poco più lento.

Gretel (rubs her eyes, looks around her, and raises herself a little, whilst Hänsel turns over on the other side to go to sleep again.)

Where am I?   Wa - king?   Or do I   dream?

How come I   in the wood to lie?

High   in the

branch - es   I   hear a gentle twittering,   Birds   are be-

gin - ning to sing so sweet - - ly; From ear - ly

dawn they are all a - wake, And war - ble their morning hymn —

— of grate - ful praise. Dear lit - tle sing - ers, lit - - tle

(turns to Hänsel.)

sing - ers, Good morn - ing!

108

110

Gretel (astonished.)

And did you al-so be-hold all this?

Hänsel (interrupting her quickly.)

Fourteen angels there must have been!

Un poco ritardando.

Hänsel.

Truly, 'twas wondrous fair! And upward I saw them

Scene II.

(He turns towards the background: at this moment the last remains of the mist clear away. In place of the fir-trees is seen the Witch's House at the Ilsenstein, shining in the rays of the rising sun. A little distance off, to the left, is an oven; opposite this, on the right, a large cage, both joined to the witch's house by a fence of gingerbread figures.)

Animato. (♩. = 60)

Gretel (holds Hänsel back in astonishment.)

float. Stand still! Be still!

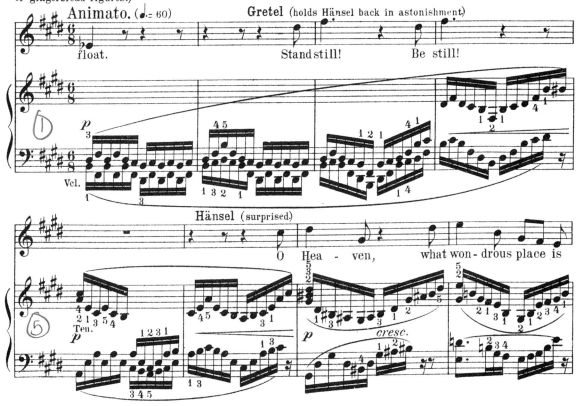

Hänsel (surprised.)

O Hea - ven, what won-drous place is

Gretel (pulling him back horrified.)

Are you quite senseless? Hänsel, howe'er can you side it!

make so bold? Who knows who may live there, in that lovely house?

Hänsel.

look, __ do look, __ how the house seems to smile! __

(enthusiastically)

Ah! __ the an - gels did our foot - steps be -

like ___ two mice ___ per - se - ve - - ring!

two mice ___ per - se - ve - - ring!

Hb.

Fl.

Vl.

cresc. - - - -

f

(They hop along, hand in hand, towards the back of the stage; - -

Trp.

ff

p

then stand still, - - - -

Hr.

f

dim. - - - -

and then steal along cautiously on tip-toe to the house. After some hesi-

p

più p

Vcl.

tation Hänsel breaks off a bit of cake from the right-hand corner.)

Scene III.

Have a care!

A

(He breaks a big piece of cake off the wall.)

lit - tle mouse your sweet - ies would share!

Fl.

fp

f

fp

fp

Gretel.

The voice from the house.

Hänsel. The

Nibble, nibble, mouse-kin, who's nibbling at my housekin?

The

Wind.

fp Hr.

dimin.

p

wind, the wind, the hea - - venly wind!

wind, the wind, the hea - - venly wind!

Vl.

Fl.

Cl.

Wind.

Str.

Vcl.

126

133

(He has in the meantime got out of the rope,
and runs with Gretel to the foreground.)

Come, sis-ter,come, let's run a-way!

(Here they are stopped by the Witch, who imperiously raises against them both
a stick which hangs at her girdle, with repeated gestures of spell-binding.)

The Witch.

Hold!

(the stage becomes gradually darker.)

Ho-cus po-cus, witches' charm! Move not, as you

fear my arm! Back or forward do not try,

Hänsel, who is gazing fixedly at the illuminated head, into the stable, and shuts the lattice door upon him.)

Ho-cus po-cus, bo-nus jo-cus, ma-lus lo-cus, ho-cus po-cus! Bo-nus

jo-cus, ma-lus lo-cus! Ho-cus po-cus, bo-nus

(The stage gradually becomes lighter, whilst the light of the magic head diminishes.)

jo-cus, ma-lus lo-cus, ho-cus, po-cus!

Molto tranquillo.

The Witch (contentedly to Gretel, who still stands there motionless.)

Now Gre-tel, be o-be-dient and wise, White

Hän-sel's growing fat and nice. We'll feed him up, you'll see my

rea_son, And with sweet al_monds and with rai-sins sea_son. I'll go in-

doors, the things to pre_pare, And you remain here where you

(She grins as she holds up her finger warningly, and goes into the house.)

Gretel (stiff and motionless.)

are! O, what a horrid

142

Now get ev'-ry-thing rea-dy and nice,   Or   else ___ I shall

389 *cresc.* - - - - - -   *f*   Str.

(She threatens and titters. Gretel hurries off.)

lock you up   too in a   trice!   He he he he he   he!

393 *f*   *dimin.* - - - - -

Molto più lento.

(To Hänsel who pretends to be asleep.)

The fool is slumb'-ring,   it   does seem

397 Cr. ingl.   Vcl.
p   *espressivo*

Bass.

queer How youth can sleep and have ___ no fear!   Well, sleep a-

400

Allegro.

good, ___ Just the thing for witch-es' food!

(She opens the oven door and sniffs in it, her face

lighted up by the deep red glare of the fire.)

The dough has risen, so we'll go on pre-par - ing.

Hark, how the sticks in the fire are crackling!

(She pushes a couple more faggots under; the fire flames up and then dies down again.)

The Witch (rubbing her hands with glee.)

Yes, Gre-tel mine, how well off you I'll dine!

See, see, O how sly!____

When in the ov-en she's peep-ing, quick-ly be-hind her I'm creep-ing! One lit-tle push, bang

148

The Witch Valse.

together, first in the front of the stage, and then gradually in the direction of the Witch's house.)

(When they get there Hänsel breaks loose from Gretel and rushes into the house, shutting the door after

him. Then from the upper window he throws down apples, pears, oranges, gilded nuts, and all kinds of

sweetmeats into Gretel's outstretched apron.)

(Meanwhile the oven begins crackling loudly, and the flames burn high. Then there is a loud crash, and

the oven falls thundering into bits.)

(Hänsel and Gretel, who in their terror let their sweetmeats all

fall down, hurry towards the oven startled, and stand there motionless. Their astonishment increases when

they become aware of a troop of children around them, whose disguise of cakes has fallen from them.)

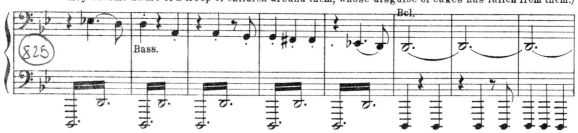

Gretel. (spoken) There, see those little children dear,
Hänsel. I wonder how they all came here!

Scene IV.

164

170

(The Father appears in the background with the Mother, and stops when he
(half spoken)

Tra la la la, tra la la la la, Ha! Why they're really there!

Vivo.

dimin.

Last Scene.

sees the children.) Hänsel. (running towards them.)

Allegro molto. (♩=120)

Fa - ther! Mo - ther!

Hr.

Gretel. (the same.) Mother. Father.

Fa - ther! Mo - ther! Chil - dren dear! O

cre -

(Joyful embracing.)

wel - come, poor chil - dren in - no - cent!

scen - do ff

(Meanwhile two of the boys have dragged the Witch, in the form of a big gingerbread cake, out of the

Un poco

ruins of the oven. At the sight of her they all burst into a shout of joy. The boys place the Witch in the

middle of the stage.)

When past bearing is our grief, God the Lord will send _____ re-

Maestoso.
Gretel.
When past bear-ing is our grief, God the Lord will

Hansel.
When past bear-ing is our grief, God the Lord will

Mother.
When past bear-ing is our grief, God the Lord will

Father.
lief! God the Lord will

When past bear-ing is our grief, God the Lord will

When past bear-ing is our grief, God the Lord will

Maestoso.

Più allargando.
molto cresc.

Più allargando.

cresc.

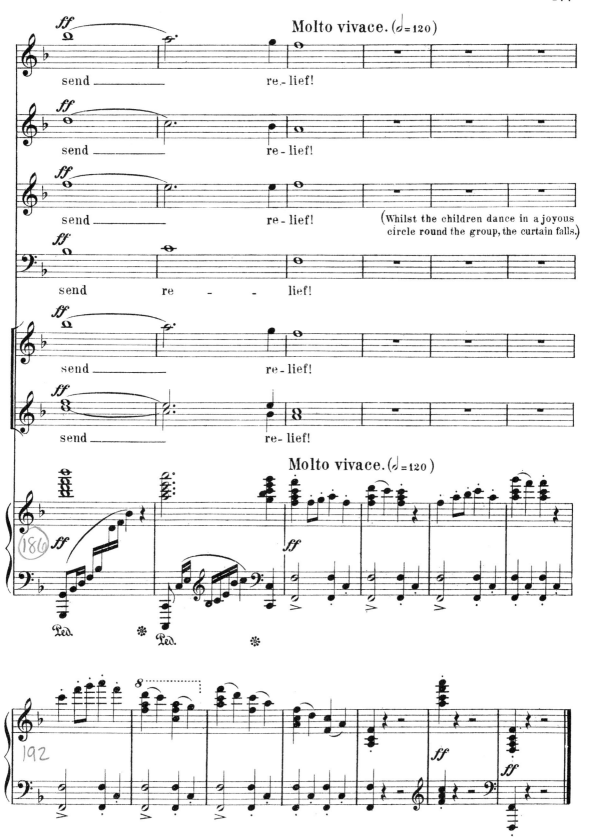

(Whilst the children dance in a joyous
circle round the group, the curtain falls.)

The End.